The Yes And Journal
An Improviser's Guide to Life

Matthew Beard

ISBN-13: 978-1978109759
ISBN-10: 197810975X

For Josh, Justin, Jay, and improvisers everywhere.
Your energy and support make this community possible.

"I am often asked, what can improvisers do in between shows and classes to get better? One thing I found that helps is to write, or more specifically, to journal.

You can work out a lot of stuff on the page that can help you get out of your own way. So, when I heard improviser Matthew Beard was creating an improv journal, I got excited."

—*Jimmy Carrane, host of the Improv Nerd Podcast*

"When you think about it, your life is more like an improvisation than any scripted play. We're always improvising, even when we are not aiming for comedy. Those who study improvisation know that the principles that give a performer confidence and guidance are also great advice for life: things like- be positive, notice the gifts, help your partner, enjoy the ride.

With this book Matthew Beard has created an amazing way to focus our minds on how to apply improv to life. His journal does something important: it gives us a way to practice improv when we are alone. I can't wait to buy a bundle of these useful books to give to all of my friends. You should too!"

—*Patricia Ryan Madson, author of Improv Wisdom*

Contents

You Are an Improviser

As I write this, I am sitting under a tree in a park, scribbling in the margins of my paper and pretending I know what I'm doing. To my right, I can hear a young couple on a first date. They laugh awkwardly in the pauses between their conversation, assuring themselves and each other that they know what they're doing too. Across the park, I see a mother shouting to her child that he should get out of that tree right now because she knows what she's doing and he had better listen. It seems to me that the only sane person here is hanging upside down from a tree branch. He seems totally happy with uncertainty, with the joy of not knowing what will happen next. When did we lose that feeling? At some point in our lives, we have all forgotten a lesson that children know instinctively:

Life isn't scripted. Every interaction we will ever have exists in the moment, with a million shifting circumstances that are entirely out of our control. We love to tell ourselves that we have it all figured out, that by this point in our lives we should *know what we're doing*. That we're grown-ups, that everyone else seems to get it. Uncertainty is scary and "planning" sounds so much nicer than "winging it", so we pretend. We fake it till we make it and leave uncertain thoughts in our heads forever. Because of this, most people are entirely convinced that improv only happens in comedy bars or college clubs.

You're different. You picked up this book. You know more than most people ever will that life happens now, and that we should not be afraid of that fact. You understand that we can practice improv skills instead of pretending that they don't exist. I don't care how much experience you have on stage — you are an improviser. This book is for you.

"On Stage" Skills and "Real Life" Skills

The distinction between *on stage* and *real life* is difficult, confusing, and frankly a waste of time. They are the same. *You* are the same in both situations. If you become a more honest, accepting, and happy person on stage — those skills will transfer into your real life. If you become a more confident, grateful, and connected person in real life — it will carry into your stage presence. The only thing mystical about being on stage is that the lights, the setting, and the audience are all giving you permission to use those skills to the fullest.

Giving Yourself Permission

This idea of "giving yourself permission" will come up again in the book. It might seem like a strange term, but we all experience it every day. When you sit in an audience and other people laugh, they are telling you "Yes, it's okay to laugh now!" When an improv instructor chooses joyful exercises, she is telling the class "Yes, it's safe to make mistakes here!" These social pressures are rarely stated outright, but they shape our decisions. They encourage or discourage our actions before we even make them.

I fell in love with improv because its focus on acceptance gives people permission to be the best versions of themselves. A good improviser sends the message that "Yes, exactly what you want to be or do or say is correct." This is such a rare feeling outside of improv, and such an important yet unnoticed aspect of our work.

That feeling is why many people think "onstage" skills don't apply offstage. When you perform, every social pressure in the room is telling you to use your skills to the fullest—those tangible, human skills like acceptance, connection, confidence, etc. These are universal skills. They're no different at home, school, work, or on stage. The context may be sending you a different set of social cues, but that's it. What if you could feel just as comfortable using those skills in any setting?

This book is about giving yourself permission to try. To stay joyful, to keep listening, and to be okay with making mistakes — on stage or off. Will this make you a better improviser? Absolutely. The skills will transfer, and the last section of this journal is full of exercises that tackle specific and nuanced techniques on stage, if that interests you. But first, I want to share what I believe this art form can be. By focusing on the skills of improv regardless of the "on-stage" or "off-stage" context, we can live better lives and become better performers in the process.

Journaling

The lessons in this book are entirely self-directed, based on written prompts at the top of each page. These prompts are inspired by what I believe to be the most valuable philosophies of improv. If you've ever journaled before, you'll know that it is an effective way to work through patterns of thought in a clear and organized way. In the words of Socrates, "I cannot teach you anything, I can only make you think." I hope that these ideas, worked out on paper, convert into real action in your daily life. You might notice that there are lots of pages after each prompt. You do not have to fill every page if you don't want to — they're just there for people with bigger handwriting. Additionally, if you find an exercise especially useful, I encourage you to rewrite it on separate paper often.

I will not be offended if you skip an exercise. That said, I would ask you to think about why you're skipping it first. Often in improv (and in life) we can learn the most from the things that give us resistance. If you find an idea or pattern of thought that shuts you down, chances are that it happens at other moments in your life too. It might even happen on stage, consciously or unconsciously. If you encounter this, I challenge you to write about why you feel that way. Give yourself permission to be vulnerable — nobody else will read this but you.

Lastly, have fun.

This art form is fun. It's insanely fun. It can be transformational, and powerful, and life changing. But, at the end of the day it should always be fun.

This journal is no different. Give yourself permission to be silly, to make mistakes, and to scribble all over it.

Alright, let's do this. Everybody circle up.

Gratitude

Gratitude is at the core of everything we do in improv. An effective workshop or performance cannot exist without it. It is the invisible energy in the room, shared through our laughter and support. We generate gratitude in our warm up games and carry it onto the stage with us. If you've ever felt valued or appreciated in improv, you've been a part of this process.

But gratitude does more than just make us feel good. It eliminates fear and creates connection. It's impossible to be afraid and grateful at the same time. It is impossible to appreciate someone without deepening your understanding of who they are. When you focus on what you love about another person, empathy connects you at the deepest level. The best improv groups use this skill to create a super-human sense of connection called "group mind."

Our culture makes it hard to express our appreciation for people, especially ourselves. For this section, give yourself permission to break through those expectations. In some exercises, it will be obvious how gratitude applies, while in others it may be subtler. Go forward with an open mind, and notice how you feel when you make this a habit.

What are you good at?
What are you proud of?

This is your journal, nobody else's. No one is going to read this except for you. So, what are you good at? What are you specifically proud of about yourself? This is no time for modesty, write everything and write it with exclamation marks. When do you absolutely crush it like nobody else? Go!

_____

_____

_____

_____

_____

_____

_____

_____

_____

_____

_____

_____

_____

_____

What are your loved ones good at?
What are you proud of them for?

Start to think about the people in your life and how incredible they are too. Try to write a few bullet points for each person, and think deeply about their skills. Extend the same gratitude to them as you gave yourself.

_____

_____

_____

_____

_____

_____

_____

_____

_____

_____

_____

_____

_____

_____

_____

_____

_____

_____

_____

_____

What are your fellow performers good at?

If you have a group of people you perform improv with regularly, use this space to write about their specific talents. List five things that you genuinely appreciate about each prson in your group or your class. Find some specific things they do that you find hilarious, captivating, or sincere.

_____

_____

_____

_____

_____

_____

_____

_____

_____

_____

_____

_____

_____

_____

_____

_____

_____

_____

_____

_____

_____

_____

_____

_____

_____

_____

_____

_____

_____

_____

_____

_____

_____

_____

_____

_____

What are you good at as a performer?

No matter to what degree, you are a performer! Use this space to write about your specific skill set and your strengths in front of an audience. Again, this is no time to be modest! In what ways do you absolutely crush it on stage? What is your style, what might other people say you do best?

_____

_____

_____

_____

_____

_____

_____

_____

_____

_____

_____

_____

_____

_____

Who do you know is supporting you right now?

Write about everyone you personally know that is making your life better. How are they doing it? In what ways are they shaping you as a person, or going out of their way to make you happier? See how many people you can list.

_____

_____

_____

_____

_____

_____

_____

_____

_____

_____

_____

_____

_____

_____

Who is supporting you that you don't even know?

Imagine all the artists, writers, and hard workers that have improved your life, all the people behind the scenes trying to make your life better. Make a list of who these wonderful strangers might be, and exactly how they help you every day.

_____

_____

_____

_____

_____

_____

_____

_____

_____

_____

_____

_____

_____

_____

_____

What is unique and valuable about the place you live?

What specific things make your city special? What about your street? Your home? Your room? Make note of the little details that you're especially grateful for. Even if you don't particularly love where you are right now, find the little moments that you can appreciate.

_____

_____

_____

_____

_____

_____

_____

_____

_____

_____

_____

_____

_____

_____

_____

_____

Write a letter of gratitude to someone you know.

Choose one person who has made a major impact on your life and send them a letter to thank them for it. Get specific and get vulnerable — you don't actually have to send the letter if you don't want to. But when you're done writing, think about how it would feel if you did.

_____

_____

_____

_____

_____

_____

_____

_____

_____

_____

_____

_____

_____

_____

Negative Visualization
—What would life be like without them?

Choose a person you know and imagine what your life would be like without them. Write about the struggles you would face, who you would be, and how it would feel if you had never known them at all. If you find yourself feeling sad or hurt during this exercise, remember what a gift they are to your life and tell them that.

_____

_____

_____

_____

_____

_____

_____

_____

_____

_____

_____

_____

_____

_____

_____

_____

Dealing with difficult people
—What can I appreciate?

Choose someone that you often have a hard time dealing with. Someone who you dislike, or at the very least, who you try to avoid. You don't have to appreciate everything about them, but for a few moments now, find something that you can. Imagine them as full, complex people with redeeming qualities. What are the things you hate to admit, but that you really could appreciate about them?

_____

_____

_____

_____

_____

_____

_____

_____

_____

_____

_____

_____

_____

Lightning round—five things

Set a timer for five minutes. Try to answer all the prompts in this section in that time. Ready? ...Go!

List five beautiful things you can see right now.

_____

_____

_____

_____

_____

List five people that you care about.

_____

_____

_____

_____

_____

List five of the coolest animals you know.

_____

_____

_____

_____

_____

List five things you love about yourself.

_____

_____

_____

_____

_____

List five goals you have accomplished in your life.

_____

_____

_____

_____

_____

List five of your favourite answers from this prompt..

_____

_____

_____

_____

_____

In Review

By this point, you should have practiced gratitude in a number of forms and gained a new perspective into how it works for you. I hope it's been a fun and helpful experience. That being said, writing is the easy part. It's much harder to go out into the world and share this gratitude with others.

For this prompt, I challenge you to take a few days and share your gratitude with as many people as possible. Tell them what they mean to you, and say it to their face. Fill these pages with stories of real life examples, then continue to the rest of the book.

_____

_____

_____

_____

_____

_____

_____

_____

_____

_____

_____

_____

_____

_____

_____

_____

_____

_____

_____

_____

_____

_____

_____

_____

_____

_____

_____

_____

_____

_____

_____

_____

_____

Acceptance

Improv is a unique art form — there is no finished product that we can chisel away at over time. Our "product" is the process of creation itself, happening live on stage in front of the audience's eyes. When we say that an improviser is accepting an offer, what we really mean is that they have agreed (verbally or nonverbally) to be a part of this process together. That they trust themselves and their fellow improviser to figure it out right here and now. Saying "Yes, and" is one form of acceptance, but so is looking your partner in the eye, or choosing to look away, or joining in on their tasking, or setting up an entirely different task of your own. *Any choice* that tells your partner "I am here with you right now in the *process* of this work" is an act of acceptance. To block an offer, then, is to deny the validity of the process—or worse—to assume that you can control it.

If our goal is to surrender our fears and our ego to the process of improv, we will need to practice. Some of the best improvisers on earth still struggle with this feeling when they step on stage. Thankfully, our lives give us hundreds of opportunities to try this every single day. We wake up to a world that is totally out of our control, and we have to do our best to figure it out as we go along. To add to the challenge, this is almost always done with other people. Life is improv. In my opinion, the greatest skill you can possess is the ability to accept the *process* of living — whatever that might mean — in any given moment.

For this section, let's practice that skill. Let's say "yes" to life. The following exercises will be focused on accepting who we are, accepting those around us, and accepting what's out of our control. By wiring this new way of thinking into our minds, we'll become better performers, but also calmer, happier people.

Optimistic pessimism—"Yes, that just happened."

Awful things really do happen to all of us. We are not helping anyone by pretending that they don't. Acceptance is not about ignoring problems, it's about saving ourselves pain and frustration by accepting that they happened. Rather than wrestling with all the things that could have been different, we should look at our problems and say "Okay. I'm here now. *What can do I next?*"

For this exercise, think of a time when something awful happened to you. With the benefit of hindsight, write about what you could have done differently if you had first accepted the situation.

_____

_____

_____

_____

_____

_____

_____

_____

_____

_____

_____

_____

_____

_____

_____

_____

_____

_____

_____

_____

_____

_____

_____

_____

_____

_____

_____

_____

_____

_____

_____

_____

_____

What do you stand for?

When times are tough, our core values can help make sense of everything. It's a lot easier to accept yourself and to accept others if you know what's important to you first. This exercise will probably take some time, but I guarantee it will be worth it. What are the values that guide your decisions? At the end of your life, what do you want to be remembered for? What are the traits you admire most in others?

Here is a list of just a few values to help you consider for yourself:

Accountability—Accomplishment—Adventure—Beauty—Belonging—Balance—Community—Consistency—Discipline—Empathy—Ethics—Faith—Family—Freedom—Generosity—Growth—Honesty—Hope—Honor—Independence—Intellect—Joy—Love—Money—Nature—Optimism—Purpose—Respect—Selflessness—Stability—Truth—Tradition—Understanding—Vitality

_____

_____

_____

_____

_____

_____

_____

_____

_____

How are you imperfect?

The phrase "nobody's perfect" is a tired cliché, but also a deeply important statement. We are all broken people. We have fears and insecurities that don't make sense, we behave irrationally towards the people we care about, and we have a really hard time understanding what will make us happy. The good news is — this is true for everyone. For this exercise, let's acknowledge the quirks that make us distinctly human. Write some of these imperfections, and next to each one, write "This is normal." Let this feel like a warm hug for yourself. You are not alone in these feelings.

_____

_____

_____

_____

_____

_____

_____

_____

_____

_____

_____

_____

_____

_____

_____

_____

_____

_____

_____

_____

_____

_____

_____

_____

_____

_____

_____

_____

_____

_____

_____

_____

_____

What would you do if you knew you could not fail?

If you had 100% certainty that you were smart enough, lucky enough, determined enough, and had all the right resources—what would you do? Would you start a business? A new artistic vision? Would you move? Make a list and really think about this. When we are afraid of failing, our dreams can shrink or be forgotten. Accept your dreams, no matter how unlikely or embarrassing they seem. What would you do if you couldn't fail?

_____

_____

_____

_____

_____

_____

_____

_____

_____

_____

_____

_____

_____

Dealing with difficult people—Experiences and Control

Choose a person you have a hard time dealing with. Someone who stresses you out, or who you often try to avoid. What experiences have they lived that you haven't? What might have shaped who they are now? You don't have to know the answer, just try to imagine how their life might be complicated too. Lastly, look to your specific example and consider what you can or cannot control.

_____

_____

_____

_____

_____

_____

_____

_____

_____

_____

_____

_____

_____

_____

_____

What stresses you out?
How much of it can you control?

Make a list of the things that stress you out. This can be anything, so try to get a list of at least 10 or 15. When you're done making your list, look back on it and write about what you can and can't control. For example, I might write that I'm worried no one will like this book. Then, I would write that I can control the time and effort I put into writing and editing, but I will never be able to control how people react to it. Make your list, and if you find things that are out of your control, try to accept what you can do and let go of the rest.

_____

_____

_____

_____

_____

_____

_____

_____

_____

_____

_____

_____

_____

Free write—"I am"

Give yourself a five-minute timer and do not stop writing for that entire time. This will come up again in the journal, and it is known as "free writing." Never take your pen off the paper, even if you start writing utter nonsense. If you ever get stuck, start a sentence with the words "I am . . ." Use these questions as inspiration, but know that you don't have to answer them all:

Who are you when you feel unstoppable?

Who are you when you feel powerless?

Who are you for your friends? Who are you for your family?

What do you love about yourself?

_____

_____

_____

_____

_____

_____

_____

_____

_____

_____

Facing regret—letter of apology

For this exercise, choose something that you regret doing or saying. It can be big or small, just choose a specific thing. Then, write a letter of apology to yourself outlining why you did what you did and how you feel. When you're done, respond with a letter of forgiveness to yourself. This might seem silly, but allow yourself to get real. You may be surprised by what you find.

_____

_____

_____

_____

_____

_____

_____

_____

_____

_____

_____

_____

_____

_____

_____

_____

Reflecting on your day—letters to a role model

Write a letter to someone you admire, even if you don't know them personally. In the letter, tell them about your day today. Tell them how you feel it's going so far, good or bad. Then, write a response letter in their voice. It does not have to be perfect, but try to imagine how they would respond. Would they be supportive? What advice would they offer?

Lightning round—Where are you from?

Set a timer for three minutes. Try to answer all these prompts in that time. If you go over, that's fine, just try to answer each prompt with the first thing that comes to mind.

I am from my hometown.

I am from _____.

I am from the street where I grew up.

I am from _____.

I am from a memory with my family.

I am from _____.

I am from my favourite meal.

I am from _____.

I am from a time that I felt loved.

I am from _____.

I am from a time that I felt hurt.

I am from _____.

I am from the thing that makes me proudest.

I am from _____.

I am from a person who changed my life.

I am from _____.

I am from my passions.

I am from _____.

In Review

Hopefully by now you have a better sense of acceptance for yourself and others. These prompts have been about saying "yes" to the process of living — a process that is not always easy. Rather than trying to control those difficult things, this section of the journal asked you to try and accept them as a normal and unavoidable part of life. You might have even found that surrendering to the moment can be a joyful process.

For this last prompt, write about what this means for you as a performer. How can you carry this sense of acceptance on stage in the way you play?

_____

_____

_____

_____

_____

_____

_____

_____

_____

_____

_____

Mindfulness

To improvise, we must have a healthy and stable relationship to our thoughts. It's very hard to be present on stage while thinking about how that last scene went, if audience likes you, or if this was the right outfit to wear today. We can never fully silence our thoughts, but we can get better at focusing them. You can practice this skill anywhere, just by sitting in the present moment and noticing it. Mindfulness is a practical tool for "getting out of your head." I'm sure I don't need to tell you that this skill makes for a better life offstage, as well.

This section is about getting into this moment. It should be a calm and joyful process, but it will also mean confronting the things you don't usually want to think about. We all have negative patterns of thought that hold us back from doing our best, and this can be especially true for performers or comedians. Try to observe these thoughts on paper without judgement and notice whether they hold up.

Now take a deep breath, relax, and write.

Brain Dump—What's on your mind right now?

Use this space to write down whatever thoughts have been lingering in your head for the past few minutes, hours, or days. Often, we get stuck in patterns of thought that we never really address. This is especially when we think about the future or the past. For a few minutes, write down whatever comes to mind. Everything you write is correct. Notice how it feels to get these thoughts down on paper.

_____

_____

_____

_____

_____

_____

_____

_____

_____

_____

_____

_____

_____

_____

_____

_____

_____

_____

_____

_____

_____

_____

_____

_____

_____

_____

_____

_____

_____

_____

_____

_____

_____

What can you hear right now?

Take a deep breath and turn your attention to the sounds around you. Really listen to all the individual noises, and write them below in the form of "I hear . . ."

_____

_____

_____

_____

_____

_____

_____

_____

_____

_____

_____

_____

_____

_____

What can you see right now?

Again, take a deep breath and turn your attention to the visual space around you. Notice the specific details, colours, and textures of the things around you, and write them below in the form of "I see . . ."

_____

_____

_____

_____

_____

_____

_____

_____

_____

_____

_____

_____

_____

_____

_____

What can you see, hear, feel, smell, or taste?

Take a deep breath and expand your awareness to all your senses. Feel your body pressing against your seat and take in the space around you. For a few minutes, write all the sensations that come into consciousness in the form of "I see . . .", "I hear . . .", "I feel . . .", etc.

_____

_____

_____

_____

_____

_____

_____

_____

_____

_____

_____

_____

_____

_____

_____

Expanding awareness to thoughts

Take a deep breath, feel your body's weight against your seat, and begin to take in the sights and sounds of the room. For as long as you would like, write what you can see, hear, and feel—but whenever a thought comes into your mind, write "I think of . . ." and record it. You don't need to analyze it or judge it, just record the thought and return to your senses.

_____

_____

_____

_____

_____

_____

_____

_____

_____

_____

_____

_____

_____

_____

Limiting beliefs
—What story are you telling yourself?

Most of us try to wrestle with our thoughts while they're still stuck in our heads, but journaling can allow us to look at them objectively. For this exercise, consider what beliefs might be limiting you as a performer and as a person. What do you believe about yourself? What do you believe about your place in your social groups? Do you think that you're funny? That you're smart? That you're worthy of attention from those you respect? Write what you believe about any of this and more, then notice if they are all based in reality.

What have you been pretending not to know?

What is a lie you often tell yourself? What have you been putting off, or refusing to think about? Take a moment to think about it now, on paper. What are your next steps? What truths do you need to accept? This exercise is not about judging yourself, it's just about going to places that might normally cause resistance.

_____

_____

_____

_____

_____

_____

_____

_____

_____

_____

_____

_____

_____

_____

_____

_____

Lightning round—five things

Set a timer for five minutes and try to answer the following prompts in that time. Ready? Go!

List five things you can see right now.

_____

_____

_____

_____

_____

List five things you can hear right now.

_____

_____

_____

_____

_____

List five things you can feel right now.

_____

_____

_____

_____

_____

Close your eyes and take five deep breaths.

How do you feel right now?

_____

_____

_____

_____

_____

In Review

This section, while shorter than the others, gives you a set of tools you can use any time. Mindfuless is a practice. If you found yourself more present, less "in your head," then I would encourage you to find time for this every week, if not every day. For these last two pages, write about the ways you can incorporate mindfulness into your improv performances and into your life.

_____

_____

_____

_____

_____

_____

_____

_____

_____

_____

_____

_____

_____

Solo Rehearsal Exercises

Now that you have experience giving yourself permission to be grateful, accepting, and present, the technical skills of improv will come naturally. You're a pro at getting yourself into the most empowering state to learn and grow, before you start to think about theory. The last section of this journal is about practicing those nuanced and stage specific skills that make for good comedy. These exercises will engage your subconscious mind by forcing yourself to keep making choices, and help you work out your specific stage presence.

If you want to get better in between classes and shows, this is a great way to do it. These prompts will be a good starting point, but continuous reflection and engaging your mind are the best way to stay sharp. Feel free to adapt my exercises and repeat them often.

Free write—Solving a made-up problem

For five minutes, write every single solution you can possibly think of to a made-up problem. They do not have to make sense, in fact most probably won't. Let your creativity flow without judgement, just have fun. This is a great way to prime your creative mind. Examples of problems: how to open a locked door, how to tear down an old barn, etc.

_____

_____

_____

_____

_____

_____

_____

_____

_____

_____

_____

_____

_____

_____

Free Write—Adopting a point of view

For three minutes, don't stop writing. Keep your pen on the page the entire time, even if you're writing nonsense. During this exercise, choose a strong *point of view* and write in the voice of that person the entire time. Examples might be: a character who firmly believes in Santa, a character who LOVES mayonnaise, etc. It doesn't have to make sense, just pick a POV and write.

_____

_____

_____

_____

_____

_____

_____

_____

_____

_____

_____

_____

_____

_____

_____

_____

_____

_____

_____

_____

_____

_____

_____

_____

_____

_____

_____

_____

_____

_____

_____

_____

_____

_____

_____

_____

_____

_____

_____

_____

Free write—Connect to an emotion

Choose an emotion that you experience regularly, either in your characters on stage or in your daily life. For five minutes, write about how that emotion feels, when you feel that emotion, how your body looks when you're in that emotion, etc. If you ever get stuck, just write the word until you think of something. This doesn't have to be ground-breaking or intense, just try to keep writing anything.

_____

_____

_____

_____

_____

_____

_____

_____

_____

_____

_____

_____

_____

_____

Free write—Absolute nonsense

For this exercise, your goal is to not make any sense. The moment a sentence starts to make sense, change it up. This will be more difficult than it sounds. For example, I might write "Caterpillars swing merrily from rooftop to antelope but the grass screams in winter." I was about to write "rooftop to rooftop," but that would have made sense, so I didn't. Try this and see if you can go a full minute or two without stopping.

_____

_____

_____

_____

_____

_____

_____

_____

_____

_____

_____

_____

_____

Free write—Write an improvised scene

Five minutes. Don't stop writing. Practice your impulse work by writing the role of both characters in a scene — write out their dialogue and any action they take in the scene. The goal here is not to be perfect or funny, just to make choices quickly. This might be hard the first time, but feel free to repeat it on separate paper again later.

_____

_____

_____

_____

_____

_____

_____

_____

_____

_____

_____

_____

_____

_____

_____

_____

_____

_____

_____

_____

_____

_____

_____

_____

_____

_____

_____

_____

_____

_____

_____

_____

_____

_____

_____

_____

_____

What are your strong opinions?
What's uniquely you?

Every improviser has a different background and worldview, and that makes for some interesting dynamics on stage. All comedy is rooted in truth—the funniest improvisers can pull from their own experiences to create specific and hilarious choices on stage. For this exercise, write all the opinions and experiences that you have which most people do not. What makes you different as a player? You can use all these on stage.

_____

_____

_____

_____

_____

_____

_____

_____

_____

_____

_____

_____

_____

_____

_____

_____

_____

_____

_____

_____

_____

_____

_____

_____

_____

_____

_____

_____

_____

_____

_____

_____

_____

_____

_____

Before a performance
—Trapping lingering thoughts

This is an exercise I do before every single performance. Five to ten minutes before you get on stage, write down every thought that comes into your head. It does not matter what it is, just write it down. Don't judge. Your brain will automatically let go of those lingering thoughts because it knows they are recorded somewhere. Try it here now, or before your next performance.

_____

_____

_____

_____

_____

_____

_____

_____

_____

_____

_____

_____

_____

_____

_____

_____

_____

_____

_____

_____

_____

_____

_____

_____

_____

_____

_____

_____

_____

_____

_____

_____

_____

_____

Your class/performance log
—Reviewing how you felt

After every class or show, I do the same exercise. I write down when I felt great about my improv and why. I try to notice the choices my scene partner and I made, and I write the specific ways I appreciate them. Then, I write down when I felt bad about my improv and why. I write about what happened from an outside perspective, without ego or judgement. This is so that I can accept that it happened and remember that we're all just playing pretend on stage — that at the end of the day it's extremely low stakes.

Keeping a record like this can put your growth into perspective and remind you why you keep doing this. It will help you let go of the "I could have done better" feeling when times are tough, and it will help you remember the "I'm the funniest person alive" feeling when you crushed it. This reflection is so important. Keep this last prompt ongoing for the next few weeks. Try to reflect every single time you do improv, and notice how it feels.

_____

_____

_____

_____

_____

_____

_____

_____

Moving Forward

Improv is a young art form. There are countless approaches to how we should play, but none of them are "correct". We're all just playing pretend on stage with whatever style makes us feel most comfortable.

In this book, I have shared the philosophy that works for me in the hopes that you can find bits of it useful. To summarize:

- Gratitude is the energy that brings our work alive.

- Acceptance is more than just a tool for good comedy, it is the process of surrendering to the present moment with your partner.

- Play is about mindfulness, which we can practice anytime.

- Journaling is a great tool we can use to break down the barriers to creativity and keep our minds sharp.

- Improv is self-development. Contexts may change, but the work of an improviser is to develop their most fundamentally human skills.

As we elevate our art form into the wider world, I believe that last point will be critically important. We must recognize the value that improv has in changing lives, not belittle it. I hope your experiences with this book have made you feel the same way.

Manufactured by Amazon.ca
Bolton, ON